D1636889

The 10 Day

Career

Cleanse

Find Your Zen at Work

BY LYNN CHANG, PH.D.

Here's to your
Career Zen!

Lynn

Printed in the United States of America

ISBN 978-1-61043-037-1

Published and distributed by
CAREER ZEN
career-zen.com

Cover design, book design and illustrations by Ryan Sponsler
ryansponsler.com

Special acknowledgment to Jessica Hagemann of Cider Spoon Stories, Dr. Jo Eckler, Dr. Deborah Wise, and Sadani Houtz for your editorial wisdom and encouragement.

Gratitude to career counseling guru Lynne Milburn, the brilliant instructors at Yoga Yoga, my work family at The University of Texas at Austin, my inspiring CAREER ZEN clients and colleagues, my partner in zen Thomas Best, and my parents Drs. Donald and Christina Chang.

zen

/zen/ noun, adjective

a state of inner peace, balance, connectedness

embodying inner peace, balance, connectedness

Table of Contents

Preface

This book comes from decades of study, research, and practice from a variety of sciences. As a counseling psychologist, I have found Cognitive Behavior Therapy (CBT) to be quite effective in helping people feel better and improve their situations. CBT stipulates that by adjusting our thoughts (including attitudes and beliefs), we can direct our emotions and behaviors towards a healthier outcome.

The field of positive psychology adds to this cognitive theory to help us cultivate meaningful lives and improve our overall wellbeing. Consciously focusing on positive experiences, engaging with others, and utilizing our strengths are some of the ways that positive psychology helps us achieve greater life fulfillment. **All of us are seeking meaning in our lives.** Rather than seeking meaning from the external world, positive psychology shows us that meaning comes from within. It's not about finding meaningful work. It's about creating meaningful work.

Other areas of research support this idea. Quantum mechanics states that our realities are based on our perceptions. What we think is "real" can change based on our belief system. Epigenetics, a new field within biology, has shown that our biological genes can adapt and change based on how our minds interpret and perceive our environments. **Our genes no longer dictate our future, rather the power of our mind dictates our genes.** Neuroscience research further demonstrates how truly adaptive our brains can be. Through neuroimaging studies now we see that the brain can actually repair, adjust, and acquire new circuitry.

Therefore, **changing our thoughts and beliefs can literally change our reality.** The 10 Day Career Cleanse is specifically designed to give you the benefits of all of these scientific discoveries in a format that is fun and simple. The emphasis of this book is not on research reports or case studies. **The emphasis is on how you can improve your workplace wellness today.** Through exploration, play, and routine you too can achieve zen.

Introduction

"Can I just stay in your office forever??" my university colleagues would ask with a childlike grin. My delighted co-workers weren't referring to my career counseling services; they were relishing in the peaceful feeling that swept over them the moment they stepped into my office. My sanctuary had became infused with good vibes, which in turn, supported me in staying in a centered, serene state.

The more I practiced at work the principles of mindfulness, yoga, holistic health, and positive psychology, the more "zen" I felt in my career. **My work with clients became more fun and effortless.** Even during tense times in the office, I could still sense lightness around me. I accepted that **every moment was an opportunity to choose fulfillment**, joy, and love. And the more I focused on these feelings, the more readily available they made themselves to me. It's been a lovely discovery; one that has benefited both my work and those with whom I work.

This book is about how you can create more zen at work. It begins with your thoughts, emotions, and actions. Through some fun and simple techniques in this 10 Day Career Cleanse, you will learn how to cultivate and maintain a sense of joyful peace no matter what.

FIND YOUR ZEN

You can begin today to cultivate more joy, peace, and fulfillment at work. Whether you love your job and want to feel less stress, or your work is less than ideal and you need a boost of positivity, these techniques are designed to make you feel better. When you feel better, you think clearer and make better decisions for yourself. This journey is about your living more authentically and free.

The 10 Day Career Cleanse is a combination of ancient **Eastern philosophies such as yoga and meditation and cutting-edge Western science in positive psychology, epigenetics, and neuroscience.** These activities have been adapted to be as effective as possible within the context of an office environment. You probably don't have an hour each day to silently meditate at work or the ability to get to the gym during every lunch break. Moreover, in our fast-paced society of go-go-go, it's not realistic to expect your racing mind to go from zero to sixty and back again. Instead, this book invites you to slow down and watch what happens if you operate at 35mph from time to time.

The 10 Day Career Cleanse is about creating an inspired new work life, regardless of where you are along your career path. You can train your brain to focus on positivity and peace based on how you choose to think, feel, and act. Neuroplasticity is the brain's ability to form new connections at any stage of life; practice and repetition strengthen these new pathways in the brain. Not only will you learn simple and fun techniques, but your daily alarms will remind you to pause and refocus.

You can train your brain to focus on positivity and peace based on how you choose to think, feel, and act.

It is in the establishment of daily routines that you will stay centered when the unexpected arises. When work gets busy, it's easy to get distracted and distressed by the details. Instead, **you may find greater productivity and higher quality of work because of these techniques.** When work plans go awry, it's tempting to get discouraged. If, however, you are anchored in your daily routines, you can clearly see what you need to let go of and what you need to address. It's possible to work under challenging conditions with ease and grace. **Work becomes zen!**

THE PROGRAM

MAIN PRINCIPLES

OF THE 10 DAY CAREER CLEANSE:

1. Have fun!
Life is too short to be miserable. Find ways to cultivate joy.

2. Take breaks
Release stress. Train your brain to be creative and productive.

3. Do less and get more done
Step into your work flow and allow solutions to come to you.

Here is an overview of your 10 day program. Notice that each day has its own theme, and offers three corresponding techniques. The first two techniques will be new to learn and try. The third technique of the day is the same for all 10 days to build habit.

	ZOOM	ENERGY	NEUROFLIX
DAY 1: INNER WORLD	INTENTION	SWAYING SEAWEED	YOUR DAY
DAY 2: CREATE TIME	BREATHE	UNTECH YOUR NECK	YOUR DAY
DAY 3: GET UNSTUCK	CHANGE GEARS	FLOOD YOUR CELLS	YOUR DAY
DAY 4: DETACH	BE LIKE SPOCK	STEP OUTSIDE	YOUR DAY
DAY 5: IMAGINE	DAYDREAM	BREAD & BUTTER	YOUR DAY
DAY 6: PLAY	CAR TALK HUMOR	DANCE	YOUR DAY
DAY 7: ALLOW	PLAN A	POWER POSE	YOUR DAY
DAY 8: GRATITUDE	BLESSING	LOVE CLOUD	YOUR DAY
DAY 9: COMPASSION	HEART MEDITATION	WATERFALL	YOUR DAY
DAY 10: GENEROSITY	PAY IT FORWARD	SHARE A CUP OF TEA	YOUR DAY

Depending on your schedule, you can choose to do any number of the suggested activities, all of which are easy and require little time. If on certain days your schedule only allows for one or two techniques, that's fine. Do stay current and actively engaged in this program. **You are training your brain to focus more on wellness and less on stress. Re-wiring your brain circuits isn't hard, but it does take consistency.**

SET UP YOUR CLEANSE

Let's get clear on what we're aiming for in this 10-Day Career Cleanse.

<u>What in your career or work life is unsatisfactory?</u>
List up to 5 things in the **Cleansing Out** column.

Now consider what would bring you joy in your career or work life.

<u>How do you want to feel at work?</u>
List these in the **Bringing In** column.

CLEANSING OUT

Ex: Not making enough money
Ex: Deadlines and stress

1. _____

2. _____

3. _____

4. _____

5. _____

BRINGING IN

Ex: Wealth and prosperity
Ex: Productivity and ease

1. _____

2. _____

3. _____

4. _____

5. _____

What you've outlined for bringing into your work life will be the focus of your cleanse. These are your Career Cleanse intentions! You can **do this cleanse program as many times as you'd like,** each time refining or modifying your focus as needed.

IT'S AS EASY AS Z.E.N.!

Each day's three activities will be labeled as Zoom, Energy, or NeuroFlix. This quick reference will allow you to pace yourself and keep yourself on schedule. Perhaps you schedule your Z.E.N. times during morning, lunch, and afternoon, respectively.

Designate time slots that work best within your parameters and preferences, and then set your alerts or alarms for each day. Use your phone, computer, or other device to keep you on task

Otherwise it's easy for the day to get away from you!

Zoom:

Get your day started on the right foot! Zoom in to focus on the specific theme and activities. By setting aside some time first thing, you're setting yourself up for success. Implement the Zoom technique within the first 10 minutes of your work day. This will set the tone and pace for your entire day. Your afternoon self will thank you!

My Zoom Alert is set for this designated time:

_____

Energy:

Due to the sedentary nature of most workplaces, it's even more important for you to tune into your physical health and energy levels. Find a natural break in your day, such as lunch or another convenient time within your schedule. If you find that your energy ebbs and flows, these techniques can help stabilize your energy levels throughout the day.

My Energy Alert is set for this designated time:

_____

NeuroFlix:

At the end of your work day, take a step back to fully take in everything that has transpired. You will learn a neuroscience technique to clear your mind. This is a symbolic way to end each work day and begin your time at home refreshed and present. Find about 10 minutes before you leave work to implement this routine.

My NeuroFlix Alert is set for this designated time:

_____

MOMENT OF Z.E.N.

At the end of each day, you'll have a chance to reflect on the concepts and techniques you learned that day. This section allows you to evaluate which approaches were effective for you, what changes you'd make for next time, and how you feel now. Along with your reflections, you can also doodle your experiences for an additional level of processing.

Doodling brings more lightness and fun to work! When you take yourself too seriously, it creates stress in your mind and body. Even if your work is serious in nature, there are ways to take yourself less seriously. The less stress you feel, the easier it will be to step into your flow.

This book invites you to doodle at the end of each day to help you reflect and process your experiences. Author of *365 Days of Doodling* Carin Channing believes that spontaneous and simple doodling is a playful way to reveal complex ideas beyond words. **Doodling is not about "getting it right" but expressing your truth through pictures.** Allow your doodles and notes to shed insight into your 10 Day Career Cleanse journey!

It will look something like this:

WHAT WAS YOUR TAKEAWAY FROM TODAY'S THEME AND TECHNIQUES?
Doodle what that looks like to you.

Doodle

OPTIMIZE YOUR EXPERIENCE

The 10 Day Career Cleanse techniques can be adapted to a variety of workplace settings. If you have your own office with a closable door for privacy, it will be easiest to incorporate these practices. If not, you can practice these activities in any spot that you can steal away for a few moments. Standing around waiting for copies is an excellent time for some career cleansing!

Whether you work in a traditional office setting full-time, or work remotely, freelance, travel, work outdoors or part-time, these Career Cleanse techniques are an invitation to you to shift your focus to positivity and peace.

 There are several guided meditations and yoga poses described in this book. You may find it easier to follow along with the videos on CAREER ZEN's YouTube channel.

When you take yourself too seriously,
it creates stress in your mind and body.

Throughout this book, you will be guided through some gentle yoga postures. You won't need to buy any fancy equipment, wear spandex, or have flexibility to do these postures. Just a willingness to breathe and relax.

Bring two items to work: Something to roll up (towel, blanket) and something to lay on (towel, blanket, yoga mat). For yoga poses on the floor, you will need a rolled up towel for stress-relieving postures and another to place on the ground.

! If you have physical restrictions, such as back injuries or pregnancy, please consult with your physician about these yoga poses. There are alternative postures offered in this book. Always be gentle with yourself, and only do what feels right for your body.

Key points about this program:

- 🐾 **DEDICATION**. Set aside a few minutes everyday to this program. **It's in the daily routine that you will start to see change.** Each minute you attend to this program is like depositing $10 into your "bank," which accrues with compounded interest. Imagine how much you'll have at the end of 10 days, 10 weeks, or 10 months.

- 🐾 **CONSISTENCY**. It's easy to get drawn into your usual work demands and tasks. By setting automatic reminders or phone chimes, you can begin to create new habits on a daily basis. What you place your attention on grows, **so let's grow your joy at work**.

- 🐾 **RESPONSIBILITY**. No one can steal your joy. Your joy is a choice to make, regardless of how challenging the circumstances. If you want to feel happy in your career, then understand that change comes from within. **Your goal is to feel how you want to feel.** Your responsibility is to stay true to your goal.

Thanks for participating in the 10 Day Career Cleanse.

Let's get started!

If you change the way you look at things,
the things you look at change.

-Dr. Wayne Dyer

DAY 1: Inner World

If you're like most people, you want to be happy. When things are going well in your life, it's easy to feel good on the inside. You might smile more, laugh more readily, and feel more optimistic about your future. **But what happens when things don't go according to plan?** When you see things that are upsetting or discouraging, it can be harder to feel assured that all is well. You might even brace yourself for continued challenges ahead, adding to more stress and worry.

The truth is that happiness comes from within. It is a conscious choice of how you want to feel and respond to your life. Try this experiment: Think of someone you love unconditionally. It could be a child, a pet, a partner, mentor, or best friend. See them in your mind's eye and imagine them with you right now. Is your heart smiling and flooding the body with happy feels? You can summon happiness anytime, regardless of your circumstances. **It doesn't matter what is occurring externally because happiness is a feeling that lives inside of you.**

This ability to choose your emotional state is an important concept in this book. You can begin to understand this idea by categorizing everything into one of two subgroups: your Inner World and Outer World.

Your Inner World is everything within your control: how you feel, act, and think. You are responsible for your emotions, not other people's emotions. You are responsible for your actions, not the consequences that follow. You are responsible for how you think, so each moment is a conscious choice. **Your Inner World is comprised of things directly within your control.** For example, in your Inner World you can choose to think, "I am so fed up with work." The things that frustrate you at work are not part of your Inner World, but your reaction to these circumstances is your Inner World.

Your Outer World is everything else around you, such as the people, environment, setting, and circumstances. Where you work, with whom you work, your projects and presentations, etc. are part of your Outer World. Your reaction to them is your Inner World. To make it simpler to remember, consider **things that originate in you as your Inner World and things that originate outside of you as your Outer World.**

DAY 1: INNER WORLD

Now imagine that your two worlds are actually mirrors of each other, reflecting off of one another. What you experience in your Inner World is often because of what is occurring in your Outer World. When you receive a compliment from a stranger, suddenly you feel flattered. You hear an earthquake has demolished several neighborhoods and it triggers sadness. This is how your Outer World can impact your Inner World. This is the default direction of your mirrored worlds. Therefore it's logical for you to assume if only this circumstance were different or that person changed, then you'd be happy. "Once I finish this big project, then I can relax;" or "Once I get that raise, then I'll enjoy my work more." Do these if-then thought patterns sound familiar?

THE BAD NEWS: Unfortunately you have little say over your Outer World. You can't control other people or external events. You can't change them to make yourself feel better. The only thing you can do is manage your own thoughts, feelings, and actions.

THE GOOD NEWS: The mirror works in both directions! If you change your Inner World, your Outer World will change as well. Your thoughts, feelings, and actions can directly influence your external circumstances and the people around you. Choose to feel fulfilled now and your work will reflect back more things that feel fulfilling. **As a recovering control freak, I found this to be quite comforting!**

Here's an example of how your Inner World can influence your Outer World. Several years ago during a meditation, the word "recognition" came to me. I began feeling recognition for my work from myself and imagining recognition from my clients and colleagues. You know what? It felt really good! It was exactly what I needed to keep going. **I went into work everyday feeling an immense sense of appreciation and recognition.** Wouldn't you know it—that year I actually won multiple awards for my work! What a wonderful example of my Outer World mirroring my Inner World. **I felt the recognition first, then I won the awards.** Not the other way around.

That's the key.

<u>You can improve your work life and situations by changing yourself.</u> Recall from the Introduction what it is that you want to bring forth in this cleanse. If you put your focus on those matters and make their resolution your reality from within, then you will come to see the reflections manifested in your work life. When you change your Inner World to align with what you truly want, your Outer World must mirror that image back to you. It's a two-way mirror and **you can absolutely impact your Outer World by changing your Inner World.**

This theory may make little sense to you, or you may not believe it to be true. That's ok. Give these techniques and activities a try anyway, and see if things start turning around. It may not happen overnight, but usually within 10 days my clients start to see a difference. If you can feel better by practicing just a few minutes a day for 10 days, imagine how much your work life will improve if you make this a part of your every day!

If you haven't already, go ahead and set your daily alarms for the Z.E.N. techniques.

when you change your Inner World, soon your Outer World changes

ZOOM: INTENTION

There is great power in setting intentions. Unlike having a goal, **intentions are more about what you would like to cultivate within** and less about striving for and achieving tasks or accolades. In yoga classes, instructors will often ask students to start with an intention. This means inviting students to tune inward and asking themselves what it is that they wish to bring into their life. Examples of intentions are to feel more peaceful, experience gratitude, be patient, or release negativity. At the beginning of class students repeat their intentions silently to themselves a few times and then let it go. What happens is this initial focus of the intention continues to work in the background while class is underway. Students shift their focus from their intention to following the instructor's cues and trying to maintain balance in every pose. Then, at the end of class, students are invited to check in with their intention. Almost without fail, **things then feel different and the intention has taken root**. It is a powerful example of how our Inner World can translate into effective change in the Outer World with very little effort required.

Start today with an intention. Based on what you outlined during the "Setting Up Your Cleanse" process, choose a specific intention. If you've been frustrated with co-workers being petty with one another, perhaps your intention is to see harmony and partnership. If you're annoyed with projects taking too long to move forward, maybe you can set an intention for efficient and productive work.

By getting clear on what you want and then letting it go, something beyond your conscious efforts helps you make your intentions a reality. You, too, can cultivate how you want to feel each day, regardless of what's going on around you.

State your intention silently to yourself 3 times, and then let it go like you're releasing a butterfly. Don't force anything, just let things happen today as they will. That's it!

Well done.

ENERGY: SWAYING SEAWEED

When was the last time you had a really good stretch? I mean the type of sweet relief that causes you to sigh aloud? The type that makes you smile from ear to ear? I'm a big believer in stretching because it keeps our bodies and minds connected and agile.

As you go through this standing pose, observe that with each move you are simultaneously stretching the body and also challenging your balance. Without judgment, notice your balance today. It may be symbolic of your work-life balance. 'Balance' is a verb and something to continuously refine over time.

Imagine you are at the bottom of the ocean. The waves above you may be ebbing and flowing, but you are in a place of stillness and peace. Things move more slowly here. The heavy waters make all of your moves measured. Consciously stretch slowly as you visualize yourself as a seaweed in this deep, still place.

Stand with your feet hip-width apart. Feel yourself firmly planted on the ocean floor, arms by your side. On an inhale, slowly raise your arms feeling the resistance of the water. Time your movement so that your hands touch overhead the moment your inhale peaks. Exhale and carefully bend your upper body to the right, giving your left 'seaweed' hip a nice stretch. Stay and breathe steadily here for a moment. You don't need to bend far to receive the effects of this pose. On an inhale, slowly return to center, timing your movement so that you reach the top when your inhale peaks. Exhale and carefully bend to the left, letting your right hip stretch a bit. **Breathe and feel this stretch**. Like a seaweed swaying in the water, return to center on your inhale, timing the movement so that when you've reached the top your inhale peaks. Slowly exhale to release your arms so that the moment your arms touch your sides your exhale is complete. Close your eyes and breathe normally here. **Notice how your body feels.** Without narration or judgment, just notice.

Do this on your own two more times. The more relaxed you are, the longer and fuller the breath will be. Notice if your second round is slower in breath and movement than your first round. And notice if your third round is even slower than the last.

Once you've completed all three rounds, take a moment to tune in. How do you feel? What effects did this stretching have on your body, breath, and thoughts?

Imagine if you could take just a few minutes every day to do a full body stretch like this. Imagine what it would feel like if you did a little stretching and breathing every time you got up from your seat today. **Your body was meant to feel good!**

This technique is adapted from cognitive behavior therapy and neuroscience. **NeuroFlix helps your brain process your entire work day,** like pressing the reset button, so that your evening can be fresh and new. It also helps you detach from your personal life for a moment, taking a step back to objectively assess your situation. **If you ever take work home with you or have dreams about your workplace this technique can help.**

NeuroFlix is also related to the practice of mindfulness, where you are encouraged to be a curious observer of life, and not take things personally but simply notice what is occurring. NeuroFlix is the ultimate technique for cleansing out the day, which is why it's suggested at the end of all 10 days of your cleanse.

> Imagine you are watching a silent black-and-white movie of your entire day, only it's been condensed down to a 2-minute film. Everything is viewed in fast-forward motion, starting from the moment you woke up through your time at work and until this very moment.

> Your brain will likely want to stop and analyze the events to sidetrack you. "What if…" or "I can't believe she…" **Don't buy into a narrative drama.** It's a silent movie for a reason. Redirect your focus and continue. You are simply watching a movie of your entire day. When you're done, smile knowing that you've cleared and reset your day. **You are now free to enjoy your personal time!**

People love this technique to consciously end their workday with a clean slate. Is it easy? Some days the NeuroFlix technique is easier to do than other days. Your brain loves to attach stories to events, and the mind especially likes to fill in the missing pieces with doubt and fear. This tendency of the brain to respond with narration explains why people have so much compounded stress in their lives and why work can feel so heavy. **NeuroFlix can be a simple antidote!**

Expect compounded benefits by the end of your 10 days!

☐ Check this box when you've completed your daily Neuroflix!

DAY 1 MOMENT OF Z.E.N.

Congrats on completing the first day of your Career Cleanse! Today you learned about Inner and Outer Worlds, how to set an intention, taking a moment to stretch and breathe, and ending your day with NeuroFlix.

Recall your initial intention from earlier today. Has anything shifted since then? Just notice. You don't need to judge the effects or make anything happen. Simply observe.

With these simple techniques and activities, you're already making change happen. It may or may not be obvious yet, but have faith that you're on the right path. You are proactively making changes to your Inner World, which will later be reflected in your Outer World.

Notes and Doodles

Here is your chance to document your reflections and reactions to the techniques from today. How do you feel at the end of Day 1? Which techniques spoke to you? Doodle an emoji and jot down your thoughts:

Happy people build their inner world;
unhappy people blame their outer world.

– T. Harv Eker

Let your life lightly dance on the edges of Time
like dew on the tip of a leaf.

— Rabindranath Tagore

DAY 2: Create Time

Have you ever thought to yourself, "If only I had more time!"
There never seems to be enough time to get everything checked off your To Do list. The pressure of fleeting seconds is the perfect invitation to slow down and take a break. Pausing just long enough can give you the pocket of time needed to release the mental grip that time has on you. From there, your sense of time will slow down and your mind can prioritize tasks with keener discernment. **You might end up getting more accomplished with less effort!**

How is this possible?

The Greeks developed **two words for time: chronos and kairos**.

Chronos is chronological clock time, which is comprised of seconds, minutes, hours, days, etc. You may be more familiar with this linear and concrete way of viewing time as it's how our watches and calendars operate. Based on this concept of time, it makes perfect sense if you've felt that there's not enough time to get everything done. Picture an hourglass with grains of sand slipping by. This type of chronos time is finite and limited. So it's true that you will never have enough time to get everything done. **But what if you had enough time to get what you need done?**

Kairos, roughly translated as "the right moment," is measured by meaningful experiences. Kairos is non-linear, eternal, and sacred. If chronos is an hourglass, then kairos is a lava lamp. Take a moment to recall a cherished memory from your past. It might be a great vacation, falling in love, or walking across the stage in your graduation gown. You had a kairos moment that had little to do with the seconds ticking by on your watch. You were fully immersed and present with the experience itself. Surely within that memory there were events that weren't so glamorous, which probably felt more like chronos time. For instance, say you travelled across the country to hear your favorite band perform. You had an hour delay when your car blew a tire, but that hardly mattered because it was the concert of a lifetime. Your face beams with joy as you relive the incredible memories from that concert. **That's the power of kairos!**

DAY 2: CREATE TIME

Begin to **mentally shift from "I don't have enough time"** to **"I need to create time"** whenever you find your work piling up and your mind racing. Creating time means deliberately carving out a moment to step into kairos mode. At first your logical mind may balk at this idea, pointing to the clock as evidence that there's no way you can fit everything in. But give these techniques a try and see what happens.

Similar to going to the gym when you're feeling tired in order to get energized, you can carve out time now to create more time later!

This 10 Day program is predicated on the idea that by taking a few short moments out of your work day, you can create space for meaningful moments to occur. These techniques are strategically designed to get you living in kairos time more often. It's in the balance between the linear and non-linear, temporary and permanent that you create zen at work.

With more kairos time creation, you may find:

✔ Clarity of what tasks need addressing and which don't

✔ Prioritizing responsibilities in order of importance

✔ Streamlining systems to maximize efficiency

✔ Noticing some things naturally get resolved on their own

✔ Anticipating problems and addressing them before they occur

ZOOM: BREATHE

Check in with your breathing right now. Notice the pace and rhythm of it. In yoga breathing exercises help steady the mind by regulating the breath in different patterns. This particular breathing exercise is an invitation to slow down time, calm the nervous system, and receive more kairos inspiration.

Three Part Breath

Sit tall with your feet on the ground.
Place one hand on your abdomen and one hand over your heart.
On an inhale,
Fill up your abdomen with 1/3 of your breath,
Fill up your ribcage with another 1/3 breath, and
Fill up your chest with another 1/3 breath.

On an exhale, slowly relax the chest with 1/3 breath,
then ribcage with another 1/3 breath, and
pull in the abdomen to complete your exhale.

Complete 4 more cycles of breath on your own.

Note : You don't need to breathe so deeply that it's uncomfortable.
Sometimes your breath will naturally lengthen with time. Let this feel relaxing and soothing.

When you've completed your Three Part Breath exercise, take inventory. How does time feel ? How does your body feel ? What is the quality of your breath ? What is the quality of your thoughts ? There is a direct correlation between how much ease is in the breath and how much ease is in the mind. Focus on staying relaxed and open for kairos moments.

Research shows this particular breathing exercise allows your body to receive
7 times more oxygen than normal!

ENERGY: UNTECH YOUR NECK

Is your posture a little more hunched over these days thanks to technology? Being on your phone and using the computer might have you unnaturally craning your neck and rounding your shoulders and upper back. This **"tech neck"** posture cuts off the natural flow of energy that runs through your body. If you have neck tension, here is an easy way to relieve the strain and get an energy boost.

(This is a yoga posture that will require the use of something to roll up and lay on, as mentioned at the start of the book. If you don't have props today or prefer not to lie on the ground, there is an alternative posture offered.)

Roll up the short edge of your towel or blanket into a 2 inch cylinder. Place it on the ground and lay on top of it so that the roll is across your back, just under your shoulder blades. If the resulting stretch feels too intense, gently roll over to your side, unfold the roll a bit to make it smaller, and try again. You want this stretch to feel good! **If you find yourself sighing with relief, then you've done it right.**

Keep your knees bent for back support. Place your arms above the roll in any position that feels comfortable. They could be out like a T-shape, bent like goal-post arms, or comfortably overhead. Whatever feels good in your body today is the right shape for you.

Close your eyes, and return to the three part breath. Inhale: one third abdomen, one third rib cage, one third chest. Exhale: one third chest, one third rib cage, one third abdomen. Repeat three times. Release your stress and **visualize more space opening up in the body.** With each breath imagine your body softening and opening, undoing all those hours of tech neck. Enjoy the sweet relief of this moment. Stay here for 3-5 minutes.

Alternative posture:

If you can't lay on the floor, stand up and clasp your hands behind your back. Squeeze your shoulder blades together as you pull your arms away from your body for resistance. Gently bring your neck back, just enough for you to feel a release. Be graceful in this movement and don't force your head to go too far. Be able to breathe fully in and out. Slowly release the head and hands. Shimmy and shake it out. Repeat with your hands clasped such that your other thumb is on top this time.

Bonus: With your hands clasped behind your back, take a wide stance and lower your torso and head towards the floor as you bring your arms up towards the sky. Let gravity untech your neck. Feel the tension release. While in this position, look between your legs and see your environment upside down. Notice and observe what it's like when your entire world is inverted. **Consciously shifting your perspective helps to expand your mind's potential and generate more creative solutions to problems.** Who knows? This reversed viewpoint might be just the nudge to do things better in a new way!

This is the technique that you learned yesterday and will be repeated at the end of each day of the cleanse. Take a moment to watch the 'movie' of your entire day. **Enjoy the show!**

☐ Check this box when you've completed your daily Neuroflix!

DAY 2 MOMENT OF Z.E.N.

Think back to the start of the day where you learned about two concepts for time: <u>chronos</u> and <u>kairos</u>. With practice, you can create a larger sense of time with the introduction of breaks and kairos moments. Today you had a chance to use your breath to calm the mind and create a fuller sense of time, spend a few minutes unteching your neck, and 'reset' your day with NeuroFlix.

It's tempting to feel overwhelmed when it seems like you're racing against the clock. Now you know an alternative way to address time. The compounded effects of taking breaks and opening up to kairos moments can yield surprising results at work! Keep it up!

Notes and Doodles

Doodle what 'time' felt like today. Note your experiences and observations.

When you realize that everything springs only from yourself, you will learn both peace and joy.

- The Dalai Lama

When we are no longer able to change a situation,
we are challenged to change ourselves.

– Viktor Frankl

DAY 3: Get Unstuck

Are you someone who feels stuck in a rut when it comes to work?
The same routine everyday: it's more of the unfulfilling parts of your life repeated over and over again. You may not know how to get unstuck; you just know you'd like a change. And because you're in a predictable holding pattern, it's harder to think outside the box and break old habits. One of the objectives of the 10 Day Career Cleanse is to disrupt old systems by introducing new ideas.

Today you're going to shake things up. When you make changes in the emotional, physical, or cognitive realms, a chain reaction begins and every realm is influenced. Yesterday you focused on the cognitive aspects through intentions. Today you'll try some concrete physical ways to easily bring more joy to your work life. For instance, if you decided to cross your legs differently right now, by the end of this sentence you would have activated a new sequence to bring something different into your life.

The purpose of the 10 Day Career Cleanse is to bring more joy and extinguish stress from your work world. It is not on exploring how to change careers, per se, though that clarity can often arise from getting unstuck and inspired again. By shaking things up a bit, you can gain more motivation and momentum to make good career choices in general!

By making some changes, even small ones, you are unconsciously telling the universe that you're ready for something new and different.

ZOOM: CHANGE GEARS

When you keep doing the same things day in and day out, you will get the same results. **Change is important for you to evolve and grow,** and when you're feeling stagnant that's the perfect time to inject some fun.

Here are some examples of small, medium, and large changes that you can make starting today. Consider how you're feeling and what steps you'd like to take to make a change. You can select any items from the list or write in your own!

Small changes:

☐ Use a different pen or ink color

☐ Listen to a new radio station

☐ Interlace your fingers the opposite way

☐ Drink a different brand of tea or coffee

☐ _____

Medium changes:

☐ Try a cuisine or food you've never had

☐ Use your mouse with your non-dominant hand

☐ Flip your schedule so your later activities are done first thing

☐ Reach out to an old colleague or friend

☐ _____

Big changes:

☐ Attend a meeting with an intention of lifting others up

☐ Respond to a work request with a kinder attitude

☐ Make somebody laugh without speaking badly about others

☐ Send a caring prayer to a co-worker you don't get along with

☐ _____

Thanks for trying out something new!

Now observe how the rest of your day goes.

ENERGY: FLOOD YOUR CELLS

 You may find it easier to follow along with the videos on CAREER ZEN's YouTube channel.

Recall from the start of your cleanse your intentions. Ask yourself right now how do you want to feel? Is it more peace, productivity, happiness, lightness? Choose the emotion that you want to cultivate today. I intend to feel more _____.

Begin by sitting in a comfortable position. Breathe deeply and fully for a few rounds of the three-part breath. Feel your body begin to relax and soften.

Place your attention on your heart. Breathe into your heart and find the place where your emotions live. Specifically, find the place where your intended emotion lives. With your breath, see if you can make this sensation stronger. **Like a fireplace bellows uses a burst of air to feed a fire, use your breath to intensify your feeling**.

Use your breathing to expand your intended emotion and fill up your entire heart. Enjoy this sensation. As you continue to breathe, the feeling becomes even stronger and more concentrated. Perhaps the intended emotion expands so much that it spills out of the heart and into your torso. Breathe and notice all the cells in your torso are drinking in this emotion. Allow your entire torso to be flooded with how you wish to feel.

Watch how your breath flows through your body, noticing your emotion swimming upwards towards the head and neck and downwards towards your shoulders, arms, and hands. Take your time to breathe here. Visualize all of the cells in your upper body drinking in this intended emotion. **Feel your entire upper body flooded with same emotion.**

Continue to breathe. Allow breath and gravity to naturally bring the intended emotions down towards your abdomen, hips, legs, and feet. Breathe and feel these cells drink in your intended emotion. Feel these cells in sync with one another and with your upper body. Notice your whole body flooded with your intended emotion.

From head to toe, you are creating your inner world with exactly how you want to feel.

Enjoy this sensation for a few more breaths. Then slowly come back into the body, come back into the room. Take a few deep breaths here and notice how you feel.

Reset your brain by watching the 2-minute 'movie' of your day. Enjoy!

☐ Check this box when you've completed your daily Neuroflix!

DAY 3 MOMENT OF Z.E.N.

It's the end of the third day of your Career Cleanse. The theme today was getting unstuck. You learned different ways to change gears, a meditation to flood your cells with an intended emotion, and cleared your day with NeuroFlix. Think back to the changes you consciously made today. **Did anything shift or seem different to you?** It's amazing how a simple act can create a profound aftereffect. Also, it's okay if nothing drastic happened; sometimes it's the subtleties that influence you later.

Notes and Doodles

Doodle a picture of yourself getting unstuck. Incorporate words or phrases that come to mind.

The difference between misery and happiness
depends on what we do with our attention.

- Sharon Salzberg

DAY 4: Detach

Imagine it's 10 minutes before an important meeting and you're about to download the presentation you've been working on for weeks. Suddenly, the computer crashes and you no longer have access to the file. Unfortunately it's not saved anywhere else and you can't access it on your phone or your colleagues' computers. In fact, tech support says it might be hours until they can come take a look at the problem. Meanwhile, everyone is waiting for you and expecting a presentation.

WHAT DO YOU DO?

Do you focus on how bad the circumstances are? "Of course this would happen to me right now. I'm supposed to have a presentation ready to go and now what am I supposed to do?"

Do you berate yourself for not knowing better? "I should have taken care of this yesterday. If I had just done this earlier, we wouldn't have this problem. Why do I keep doing things at the last minute?"

Do you worry what others might think? "I can't afford to look bad in front of everyone. I can't believe I messed up on such a simple task. They're going to think I'm stupid."

How you respond to moments like this is related to what part of the brain you are accessing. **Your brain is comprised of a primitive portion and a newly evolved portion.** The old (primitive) part of your brain manages your emotions and survival instincts like hunger, fatigue, and breathing. The new part of your brain (the cerebral cortex) evolved later as a way for you to plan, organize, problem-solve, and reason. If you think about it, work is paying for the temporary usage of your cerebral cortex. Your advanced reasoning and problem-solving skills, not the fact that you can eat and sleep, are probably why you were hired!

The thing is, the **new brain works best when the old brain feels safe and free from danger**. It's all too easy for your everyday deadlines, inconveniences, and to-do lists to get artificially elevated to 'life is in danger' status when such 'emergencies' really require more objectivity and concentration. In the earlier example, not having the presentation ready in time for the meeting can trigger fearful thoughts, shallow breaths, and an elevated heart rate. Your old brain kicks into danger mode and suddenly it's harder to create possibilities for better solutions.

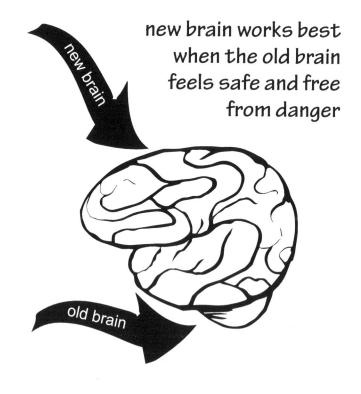

new brain works best when the old brain feels safe and free from danger

new brain

old brain

What would be an alternative way to respond? Maybe instead of having a polished presentation to show at the meeting, you explain the situation and decide to make your presentation more interactive, replete with group brainstorming and discussion. Getting the group more invested in your process can make your contributions to the project that much more meaningful. Or maybe the agenda shifts and your presentation is tabled until the next meeting. Or how about something radical? Just cancel the meeting! Have you ever seen someone disappointed that he doesn't have to sit through another meeting?

Today you'll learn some great techniques for detaching yourself just long enough to get your primitive and advanced brains back in sync. **Having a whole brain at work can stimulate concentration and productivity.**

ZOOM: BE LIKE SPOCK

Mindfulness is about being an objective observer who is curious and interested in what's going on, without emotional attachment. Temporarily detaching allows you to clearly see things without bias or assumptions. It's when you get attached to an outcome or become too personally involved in things outside of your control that you feel the stress rise. For instance, when you do your best at work and the result is a lukewarm reception to your efforts, how do you feel? If your focus relied on how your team responds to your work, then emotionally you are at the mercy of the Outer World. Conversely, if you know that you did your best, then reactions from others become feedback and data to consider, not a value statement of your abilities. **Remember that you have no control over the consequences of or reactions to your behavior.**

An easy way to stay in objective appraisal of situations is to channel your inner Spock. This popular Star Trek character was known to say **"fascinating"** whenever something unexpected happened. Preferring to stay logical, Spock came to better understand problems without strong emotions impacting his judgment. When you are able to take a calm step back, you can more accurately assess the situation and come up with better solutions.

The more stressed you get, the harder it is for your new brain to focus on helpful possibilities and productive ideas. If you're not careful, your old brain gets so worried that it takes over. Avoidance behaviors, such as excessive shopping, TV watching, eating, or drinking, then become your sole coping mechanisms. But when you can take a breather, and just observe the situation as-is, you come to see things as they really are. That is the time to re-engage with your emotional presence and come back to your whole self.

You are invited to think like Spock today. The next time something stressful arises or something unexpected happens, say "fascinating" and take a deep breath.

You only have control of your own behavior, thoughts, and feelings.

DAY 4: DETACH

Note some examples of stressful situations today and put this technique to work! Write down the situation, your initial reaction, the Spock analysis, and then your resulting action.

Ask yourself:

➡ What is actually occurring?

➡ What events have led to this moment?

➡ What needs to be remedied, if anything?

➡ What could help the situation?

The next time something happens at work and you're tempted to get overly stressed about it, remind yourself to be like Spock. Feel your mind expand and offer you alternative solutions to consider. Everyone will wonder how you learned to handle pressure so well. You can thank Spock for that!

ENERGY: STEP OUTSIDE

How often do you have conversations with yourself that start with "I need to" or "I should have?" Because your work asks for your advanced thinking mind, it's so easy to stay stuck in that mode of endless list making. Your mind and body are meant to stay connected, and the easiest way to re-connect is through nature. Take a walk outside today, and see if you can detach from stress and regroup.

There is something grounding about tuning into Mother Nature's rhythms. She reminds you that the pulse of the earth echoes in you as well. Find a few minutes to step outside for some nature time. Whether you work behind a greenbelt or in the middle of downtown, leave the indoors for a 5-minute walk outside. Notice the air outside. What does it look like or smell like? How does the temperature of the air feel against your skin? If you look up, what do you see? What if you look down? Allow nature to surprise you. Mother Nature is everywhere!

Take a couple of minutes to watch the 'movie' of your day.

☐ Check this box when you've completed your daily Neuroflix!

DAY 4 MOMENT OF Z.E.N.

Yay! It's the end of your fourth day. The theme today was detaching temporarily so that you could more effectively process what was needed at the time, especially in stressful situations. You learned how to problem solve like Spock, how helpful a walk in nature can be, and how it feels to end each day with NeuroFlix.

Notes and Doodles

How did 'detachment' impact you? Doodle what you detached from today.

You may say I'm a dreamer
but I'm not the only one.
I hope someday you'll join us,
and the world will live as one.

- John Lennon

DAY 5: Imagine

Welcome to Day 5! Yesterday you examined the ways temporarily detaching from your work world can help you de-stress and work more effectively. Detachment is a good mental exercise for your brain. And the more you practice it, the stronger the neural connections you make and the easier these techniques become.

Today you're going to take it to the next level by freeing up space in the mind and letting your imagination flow. Look around you and notice if your current situation is dictating how you feel. "Immediate circumstances" is the most common reason we feel the way that we do. **If we like what we see around us, we feel happy. If we don't like what we see around us, we feel crappy.** Going back to the mirror analogy from Day 1, recall that your Inner World and Outer World are always reflecting one another. Today is an invitation to change your Outer World by using the power of your Inner World's imagination.

What comes to mind when you see the word imagination? Perhaps it is children playing pirate games in their backyard, or artistic creations fit for a museum. **The most wonderful things in the world began with a mere thought.** And each moment you have is an opportunity to create something new in your life. It is important and healthy for your brain to continually create new connections in order to stay sharp and even subconsciously map out new routes to success.

According to holistic health expert Dr. Deepak Chopra, creativity lives in the space between your thoughts. But how many thoughts do you have and how much space is actually between them? If you're like most people, you have a continual stream of thoughts, many of them might be critical or judgmental. Giving yourself time to slow your thought processes down provides more space for new ideas and inspiration to form. **Not forcing yourself to arrive at a solution is often when your mind works best.** Allowing any rigid thought patterns or old belief structures to rest a moment can have a wonderful ripple effect on everything else. Consider this an invitation to your hardworking brain to be a kid again, if just for a moment today. Watch what happens.

ZOOM: DAYDREAM

One of the simplest ways to create a new reality is by daydreaming. When you daydream, you use your imagination to freely design a world that is interesting, fun, exciting, and completely customized by you! Your mind is finally not restricted by "have-tos" or "shoulds." You may find it actually quite liberating! Feel free to let your ideas morph and wander in any direction. Daydreaming can help you feel lighter, and when you feel lighter on the inside, the world around you feels lighter.

Set a timer and spend two minutes daydreaming.

Daydreaming is your time to allow your imagination to flow freely, to let the juices spill into other areas of your life. The more you daydream, the more endorphins your body produces and the better you'll feel overall. You will actually have a better feeling day because of this two-minute activity. And when your Inner World feels better and better, your Outer World cannot help but match it. This is how the universe will respond to your internal shift.

Word of caution: It's at this point where your rational mind might want to interfere with your feel-good process. You might have thoughts such as "But that would never happen in reality" and then what happens? You block the flow of imagination and go into rigid thinking again. Your energy will decrease and you might end up feeling stuck again. So quiet the negative thoughts and give daydreaming a shot. It's worth trying!

"A GREAT HISTORICAL FIGURE COMES BY TO OFFER ME ADVICE"

"I'M AN EAGLE SOARING ACROSS THE MOUNTAINS"

"I JUST RECEIVED A 300% RAISE. WHAT NOW?"

"MY FAVORITE VACATION SPOT IN THE WORLD IS..."

ENERGY: BREAD & BUTTER

Got neck or back tension? Want to learn a simple and effective stress reliever?

Find a place where you can lay on the floor for a little while in privacy. If needed, place something on the ground like a yoga mat or blanket. Roll up the long edge of your blanket or towel so that it's a firm 3-4" cylinder. Place the roll vertically behind you (parallel to your spine). With your knees bent, sit on the bottom edge of the roll and slowly lay down on it. Allow your head to rest comfortably on the roll. If your roll is short and your head touches the ground, scoot down so that your head is resting on the roll.

This posture should feel great immediately. It releases tension from your neck and back, improves breathing, calms the mind, and stretches the chest. You can place your arms out in a T-shape, bend them like goal posts, or rest them on your abdomen. Knees can stay bent to support your lower back.

From this position, close your eyes and **imagine you are a stick of butter and you're laying on a warm baguette.** With each breath, soften into the baguette. Allow yourself to melt more and more with each inhale and exhale. Stay for 5-10 minutes here.

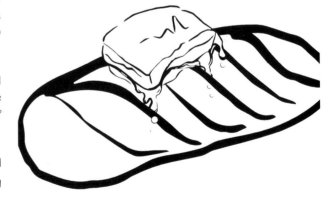

To release, gently turn to one side and remove the roll behind you. Then come back onto your back to reset the spine. Notice the difference. Is more of your back in contact with the earth? That's your body relaxing and expanding! Good job!

If your flooring situation at work is not ideal, practice Bread and Butter first thing when you get home. It's a relaxing and nourishing way to begin your personal time.

Alternative to Bread & Butter: ANGEL WINGS

This posture brings movement to your arms and shoulders, and can be done seated or standing. Allow your imagination to bring in more love into your heart and to share the love with everyone.

Begin with your hands in prayer pose, palm against palm at your heart center. On an inhale, raise your arms over your head. On an exhale, spread your angel wings wide as you lower your arms to your side and back into prayer pose. Repeat this posture five times, breathing and moving slowly. As you inhale, imagine sending love from your heart to the sky. And as you exhale, imagine your angel wings spreading the love all around you and back into your heart.

Clear the contents of your mind by watching the 2-minute 'movie' of your day.

☐ Check this box when you've completed your daily Neuroflix!

DAY 5 MOMENT OF Z.E.N.

How did your day go with a little dose of imagination? Were you able to be transported to another place, if just for a moment? It's healthy to be able to jump back and forth between your current reality and vividly-imagined alternate realties. Think of it as brain hopscotch. Envisioning success and fulfillment is how we move our Inner and Outer Worlds in a more positive direction.

Now that you're at the halfway point of the Cleanse, recall what your Career Cleanse intentions were at the start of the program. Has anything changed since Day 1? Is there anything in particular you'd like to "Bring In?" If so, set a silent intention right now and then let it go. Have gratitude that the seeds of intention have been planted.

Notes and Doodles

You are halfway through the 10 Day Career Cleanse program. **Doodle an emoji** that represents how you're feeling now.

Angels can fly because they can take themselves lightly.

- G.K. Chesterton

DAY 6: Play

Congratulations! You're halfway through the program! Already you have covered ways to redirect your attention and thoughts, change up behavioral patterns, create more time, and open up to your imagination. All of these techniques coalesce in today's focus: play!

We tend to take our work too seriously. In her book *The Five Regrets of the Dying*, palliative caregiver Bronnie Ware shares that hospice patients regret working too hard. They wish they had reprioritized their own happiness and time with family over the "treadmill of a work existence." So for you, getting a project completed before the deadline may feel like the most important thing in that moment, but in the grand scheme of things … is it really?

An important lesson to embrace is to just laugh at life!

By introducing more play into your workdays, you will naturally sense greater kairos time and begin to prioritize tasks better. Every office has its complexities, system issues, and politics. Rather than waiting for things to get better (Outer World), start enjoying your work now (Inner World). Rise above the petty and focus on what you value.

Play can take on many forms. **I once helped someone prepare for a job interview by filling both of our mouths with frozen grapes.** After a lot of traditional practice runs, I thought we would change the pace and ease the stress of the situation via this silly tactic. I "interviewed" him with questions and sounded absolutely ridiculous. He used his well-practiced answers on me and sounded equally ridiculous! Instead of feeling nervous and self-conscious, he had a hard time suppressing his giggles. By the end of the mock interview, we were both crying from laughing so hard. Needless to say, he aced the interview the next day! Look what can happen if we take ourselves less seriously.

At the end of the day, you have to laugh at life. This journey that you're on is filled with absurd situations and circumstances. Detach, and don't take it personally or too seriously.

ZOOM: CAR TALK HUMOR

<u>I know nothing about cars, yet my favorite radio program is Car Talk</u>. The award-winning car-repair show aired on NPR for 30 years, and was hosted by two brothers who were automotive experts. Over the years, thousands of people called in seeking car advice from them, and in their own unique, playful way, Tom and Ray Magliozzi entertained us with their responses. They are hilarious to listen to because they didn't take themselves too seriously and they didn't take life too seriously.

It's no wonder why callers loved talking to them. The Magliozzi brothers were down-to-earth, non-judgmental, intelligent, and wise. Despite being experts in their field, they always chuckled about not knowing anything. Being "unencumbered by the thought process" was their self-deprecating way to explain how they arrived at their conclusions. They proudly declared themselves unintelligent! How often do you worry about making mistakes in front of colleagues? It takes a lot of energy to "keep it all together" when you're shamefully trying to hide something. What if you took the opposite approach and openly joked about your innate flaws? Showing others your vulnerable side can give them permission to do the same.

Tom and Ray could take an ordinary call about a transmission and find the humor, heart, and philosophy in the underlying story. See if you can adopt their perspective and make work fun and playful. Although the retired Car Talk show is only available on podcasts, their workplace laughter inspires me every single day! And keep in mind that I know nothing about cars.

Being "unencumbered by the thought process" was their self-deprecating way to explain how they arrived at their conclusions.

You may be wondering how to implement this approach if there are complex office politics where you work. **Remember that workplace politics are never personal.** The office is a closed system of actions and reactions. Can you step beyond it and observe it as an outsider? Can you detach yourself from your work and simply imagine you're watching a cartoon? **When you can separate yourself from a situation, and look at things with humor and grace, it puts life into perspective.** You can actually do your job better because you're not caught up in the drama. Maybe letting loose a chuckle at how ridiculous life is can help make things feel lighter. **If all else fails, laugh at yourself!!** That's what Tom and Ray would say!

Today identify a situation in which you're tempted to take offense or get upset. Then detach and try to see the humorous lighter side of yourself. Your work may be serious and need to be taken care of responsibly, but you can still take yourself less seriously.

Write down what the challenging situation was, how you shifted your perspective, and the end result.

⇨ **Challenge:**

⇨ **Perspective:**

⇨ **Results:**

If all else fails, laugh at yourself!!

ENERGY: DANCE

Professional dancer and stretching instructor Miranda Esmonde-White says that when you stretch a specific part of the body, like your arms, it sends messages to the brain to release tension in that particular area. But when you stretch the hips, this action confuses the brain. It isn't sure what part to release, so it relaxes the whole body. Maybe this anatomical fluke is why dancing feels so freeing!

Today you are invited to dance at work! Give yourself the gift of a **2-minute dance party** in the middle of your office. Find your favorite upbeat tunes and dance your heart out. It's excellent cardio and emotionally uplifting. See if dancing naturally brings out a smile or two! It can feel so good to be silly and release any tension that's been building up.

TIP: Check out **'William Tell Overture Just Dance'** on YouTube. So fun!

Doodle how you felt before dancing:

Doodle how you felt after dancing:

Have fun while watching the 2-minute 'movie' of your day!

☐ Check this box when you've completed your daily Neuroflix!

DAY 6 MOMENT OF Z.E.N.

Today you focused on play. Were you able to laugh a little bit more? Take yourself less seriously? How did it feel to take a few minutes to dance in your office? By using a lighter approach you can actually improve your performance at work. As important as your job is, the feeling of mounting stress can negatively impact your cognitive abilities and emotional regulation. Hopefully these techniques will help you shift from heaviness to heavenliness!

Notes and Doodles

What was your favorite playful moment of today? Jot down phrases that come to mind or doodle what it looked like.

Some of us think holding on makes us strong;
but sometimes it is letting go.

— Hermann Hesse

DAY 7: Allow

Welcome to Day 7! Yesterday your focus was on play, incorporating more lightness and fun into your work. Now what if you only had to "do" a fraction of your current work in order to get everything done? Would you have more energy for other areas in your life? Would you be more excited about going into work?

I distinctly remember the moment when all of these career cleanse techniques came to a head and I really stepped into a divine rhythm with the universe. I was able to produce quality work with a fraction of the effort normally required. My productivity was stellar and I didn't even break a sweat. I infused as much fun, play, and imagination as possible and it totally paid off.

As was typical for a university career counselor, I was sitting across from a student and listening to her concerns about major and career decisions. She was very worried about making a mistake, and I was busy thinking of how to best explain the decision making process while reassuring her that it would all work out. When all of a sudden, I heard profound words came out of my mouth. These words were compassionate and wise, stated in the exact way that my student needed to hear them in order to best help her. **DAAAAAAAMN, THAT SOUNDED GOOD!** I thought to myself, and my student gave me a look that suggested the same. You know what? Those words came directly from a divine source. They had bypassed my brain, which was busy analyzing what the student was saying and trying hard to figure out what I should say next. Turns out the best thing to "do" was to simply allow my body to be a messenger from the universe. That's how I've been approaching my work ever since—and my work now feels lighter and exponentially better than before!

Step 1: Play to free up stress in the body

Step 2: Imagine to make space between your thoughts

Step 3: Allow divine wisdom to come through you

DAY 7: ALLOW

Today is about letting go of some effort and allowing a larger force to do the heavy lifting. What if you could get better results at work by doing less and surrendering more? There's a delicate balance between doing your part to achieve what you want, and allowing the universe to guide you in ways you didn't know possible.

Have you ever experienced an initial disappointment in not getting what you strived for only to receive something that was actually better? It's your job to get clear on what it is that you desire, get in alignment with your Inner World thoughts, emotions, and actions, and then surrender to what will be. When you learn to work within this process, the most wonderful, unexpected things can happen.

TO-DO LIST

Done!	Task	Deadline
☐		
☐		
☐		
☐		
☐		
☐		
☐		
☐		
☐		
☐		
☐		
☐		
☐		
☐		
☐		
☐		

Plan A or Plan B?

ZOOM: PLAN A

Many years ago I had the pleasure of attending a training by the late Dick Bolles, author of *What Color Is Your Parachute?* Did you know that in addition to being a celebrated career-guidance author, he also had a Masters degree in theology? He was the first person to help me connect career counseling with spiritual guidance. I distinctly remember Mr. Bolles chuckling at people who were upset when they weren't able to complete their to-do lists. He said that people think their to-do list is Plan A when it's actually Plan B. What the universe gives you is Plan A. He went on to explain that when you get a phone call in the middle of a meeting, or when a colleague needs your help immediately, or another project pops up that requires your attention, that **these "interruptions" are actually Plan A. That's the universe's plan for you; not what you write down on a piece of paper!**

What if you viewed your schedule for today as what your day could look like, but left room open for divine improvisation? Might you be more curious about what was to come rather than be stressed out by an unexpected event? Try this way of thinking and notice how you feel at the end of the day.

Make note of what your Plan B is (your scheduled day). And then stay curious as to how your day actually evolves!

ENERGY: POWER POSE

Sometimes the stress of work can leave you feeling ineffective, drained, or unbalanced—or all of the above! **Let yourself feel more solid about who you are and where you stand in the world.** Get refocused so that you can confidently do your part at work and also stay open to the universe guiding you along.

Power poses are postures that you hold in the body for 2-3 minutes to send messages to the brain about how you want to feel. Maybe you want to feel ready to take on what life gives you. Or maybe you want to feel secure in knowing that all is well. **Superheroes are a fun way to channel a positive vibe.** Which superheroes do you admire? What poses do they strike that emanate power from within? Is it a wide stance with arms on hips? Is it flying through the sky with a flapping cape? Notice in all of these superhero poses that their chin is lifted, heart is open, and feet are grounded. Try out different variations and see how you respond! Which ones make you feel the most powerful?

TIP: Try enhancing your power pose by humming a superhero theme song. Imagine how uplifting this can be right before a job interview or big presentation!

Enjoy the 2-minute 'movie' of your day. Let go of your work day.

☐ Check this box when you've completed your daily Neuroflix!

DAY 7 MOMENT OF Z.E.N.

How did your day go? Today you compared your scheduled Plan B with the Universe's Plan A, struck a power pose or two, and reviewed the contents of your day with a Neuroflix film. What did you notice about allowing your day to unfold rather than getting caught up in the "shoulds" and expectations of the day?

Notes and Doodles

'Allowing' can have many layers to the process. Doodle yourself in your favorite power pose. How did it feel? What did you learn from this experience?

Gratitude unlocks the fullness of life.
It turns what we have into enough, and more.
It turns denial into acceptance, chaos to order,
confusion to clarity.

– Melody Beattie

DAY 8: Gratitude

What has gone right today? Is this an unusual question? Think about it: since you woke up today, what things have gone well? Did your bed keep you warm and safe or did it collapse in the middle in the night? Did the flowers and trees stay rooted in the ground or did they spring up and float away? Did someone throw popcorn at you as you entered the office today? (This actually happened at a job interview!)

It is all too easy to grumble about work and find things that annoy or frustrate you. If you look around, you can probably name a dozen ways that work could be better. But what would happen if you changed your perception so that your focus were on seeing what's going well, what is actually good? Soon, you would notice that there are more things going right than are going wrong. From this place, you'll have the energy and drive to make things even better.

For the past 30 years, talk show host Oprah Winfrey has recommended keeping a daily gratitude journal to identify people, things, or experiences for which we feel grateful. The power of gratitude comes from the idea that your reality is based on your perceptions and your belief system. **What you pay attention to influences your emotions and behaviors, which creates your life day by day.** In other words, your Inner World guides your Outer World. While it can seem challenging to shift your attention to something positive when you're feeling less than satisfied, setting aside a gratitude moment can be just the momentum needed to have a fantastic work day.

Designate a time every day to practice your daily gratitude moment. Perhaps it is the moment you step into your work space. Even if you've had a rough start to the morning, this daily practice can empower you to shift things in a direction that helps you stay strong and positive all day.

You are training your brain to focus on what's going right. Take a look around you and identify what you appreciate. Really feel this gratitude. You'll notice a difference in the quality of your days when you truly emote this appreciation, as opposed to going through the motions and mindlessly listing out your gratitudes. Your daily practice can help you to finely sculpt your ideal world into being.

Every day, think as you wake up,
today I am fortunate to have woken up,
I am alive, I have a precious human life,
I am not going to waste it.
I am going to use
all my energies to develop myself,
to expand my heart out to others;
to achieve enlightenment for
the benefit of all beings.
I am going to have kind thoughts towards others,
I am not going to get angry
or think badly about others.
I am going to benefit others
as much as I can.

– The Dalai Lama

I have a Tibetan scroll with this Dalai Lama quote hung above my bathroom sink. It's a beautiful way to begin the day. How often do you wake up to a mental list of what you have to get done and then feel your heart dreading the day as a result? What would it be like, instead, to begin each day with a thoughtful approach like quote? You are setting intentions, you are feeling gratitude, you are wishing well for others. It doesn't get more profound than that!

Place the image of this scroll somewhere on your desk so that you can glance at it from time to time today. Let it be your intention. Hear the Dalai Lama's voice reading this passage to you. Allow the feeling of gratitude to wash over you again and again.

ENERGY: LOVE CLOUD

 You may find it easier to follow along with the videos on CAREER ZEN's YouTube channel.

This visualization incorporates the use of gratitude, imagination, and intention. You are encompassing the feeling of love and appreciation until it creates a **protective cloud all around you**. Regardless of your external circumstances, **you will remain securely surrounded by the power of love.**

Sit in a comfortable position and either lower your gaze softly to the ground or close your eyes. Take a few deep breaths to get centered.

Take a moment to say thank you to all the things that have gone well today. Think back from the beginning of your day until now all the things you are grateful for. Really feel a deep sense of appreciation here.

With your breath, grow this feeling of gratitude. Like a bicycle pump inflating a tire, watch how your breath grows your gratitude from the center of your heart, to throughout your body, to all around you. Breathe in gratitude, exhale expansion. Breathe in gratitude, exhale expansion.

With your breath, create a cloud of gratitude, appreciation, and love around you. **A love cloud**. See and feel the contours of this cloud around you. From this point on, know that each breath you take comes directly from this place of gratitude. This cloud will keep you protected and centered throughout the day.

Now slowly come back into the room, come back into your body, come back to your breath. Wiggle your fingers and toes. When you're ready, slowly open your eyes.

Clear your mind by watching the 2-minute 'movie' of your day. Feel gratitude for another day done!

☐ Check this box when you've completed your daily Neuroflix!

DAY 8 MOMENT OF Z.E.N.

The theme today was gratitude and focusing on what was going right for you. For some people this practice can feel unnatural and forced, and for others it can feel instinctive. You are creating new neural pathways in your brain, and with repetition and practice these pathways will become your dominant way of thinking. Imagine filling every day with what's right, creating a love cloud of around you, and giving you security to be your very best at work.

Notes and Doodles

Doodle what you are most grateful for. What surprises emerged as a result of the techniques today?

Our task must be to free ourselves
by widening our circle of compassion
to embrace all living creatures and
the whole of nature and its beauty.

— Albert Einstein

DAY 9: Compassion

Welcome to Day 9 of your 10 Day Career Cleanse! Whether you realized it or not, you have been consciously reprogramming your mind to focus on <u>gratitude</u>, <u>creativity</u>, <u>openness</u>, and <u>peace</u>. **You are coding and rewiring your neural circuitry to bring more zen into your workplace**. This process is important because by default we're operating out of our subconscious 95% of the time. Downloaded by the age of 6, each of us has a set of behavioral scripts that run on autopilot whenever our subconscious is triggered or stressed. Making decisions out of fear, needing to be liked, or feeling inadequate are examples of this subconscious programming running in the background outside our awareness. You may have observed behavior in yourself or your co-workers that seems immature or illogical. This is what happens when we're not conscious of our thoughts, feelings, and actions. **Be patient with yourself and others. We're all on this journey together**.

It's easy to feel compassion when you're with loved ones. But what about with co-workers? Your heart has an amazing capacity to connect deeply with those around you. Work can be a stressful place and it's common to feel the fear of "not enough": not smart enough, not talented enough, not good enough, not technical enough, not creative enough, etc. <u>As much joy and beauty as there is in this world, there is also pain and suffering.</u> This is the yin and yang of your existence and this is what it means to be a human being on this planet. You were meant to experience the ups and downs with your fellow brothers and sisters, supporting each other along the way.

> ## Ask: Who needs compassion today?
>
> ### Who is it easy to share compassion with?
>
> ### Who is it hard to share compassion with?

One way to know if you're running off your subconscious scripts or conscious reprogramming is to tune into the heart. Connect with an openness and curiosity about that tender part of yourself. It's the doorway to authentic relationships with and for all living things. **Those who are the hardest to love are usually the ones who need compassion the most.** Before engaging with coworkers verbally and emotionally, see if you can take a step back and see them for their humanity. Detach with compassion. Everyone is trying their best with where they are and what they have. If you've been slighted and wronged in the past, understand it was not personal. It was all about them, not you. Today's theme is about sharing compassion with people at work, beginning with yourself.

ZOOM: HEART MEDITATION

 You may find it easier to follow along with the videos on CAREER ZEN's YouTube channel.

This meditation is an invitation to keep the circulation flowing, giving and receiving compassion in a simple yet profound way. Just your intention of sending someone a kind thought is enough. You don't need to analyze who is deserving of compassion, as everyone is. **At our core, we are all living beings who want peace and acceptance.**

With your elbow bent, hold up your right hand parallel to your heart so that your palm is facing outward. This symbolic gesture allows energy to come through your heart and extend out to others. With your elbow bent close to your hip, hold up your left hand so that your palm is facing upward. This symbolic gesture is about receiving energy from others back to you. Feel how the position of your hands feed and balance each other.

Now close your eyes and take a few deep breaths to get grounded. Recognize the individuals around your immediate environment. They could be colleagues down the hall or supervisors next door. Find where compassion lives in your heart and energetically send compassion out from your hand into their hearts. Visualize this process.

Now send compassion to everyone within a one-block radius from you. Share compassion with all of them. Allow your right hand to broadcast kindness into all of them. Continue by expanding your circle of compassion to everyone in your city. This includes not only every person and his or her loved ones, but also the animals and plants. Show compassion for all living things that are striving toward the fullness of life. Shine enough energy from your right hand to send kindness and compassion for all living beings in your city.

DAY 9: COMPASSION

ZOOM OUT. Breathe. Watch as your compassion expands even more to include all living beings in your entire state. Every individual, every animal, every blade of grass ... send out compassion. **ZOOM OUT** further. Watch your heart compassionately hold space for everyone in your country. Breathe in kindness, breathe out compassion. Notice as your hand sends out energy exponentially to include neighboring countries, the other continents, and the oceans and seas. Soon your compassion touches upon every life form, from the bottom of the ocean floor to the highest mountain top. Breathe knowing that you're sending compassion for every living thing on this planet. Notice how your whole body feels. Notice how your skin feels and the fine edge between where you end and the rest of the world begins.

Now, reverse the process. It is your turn to receive the compassion from everyone around you. From your receiving left hand, take in the compassion from all beings at your workplace and in your vicinity. Let in even more compassion as you focus on all living beings from your city and state sending you love. Openly receive this compassion and feel your left hand getting heavier from this process. Notice the living beings in your country and neighboring countries sending you love and compassion. Breathe it in, and let your heart deepen from this kindness. Simply sense the kindness and compassion from everyone reaching out to you, from every continent, and **feel your receptive hand taking it in.** From the depths of the ocean floor to the tops of the mountains, all beings across the globe are sending compassion your way. This is what it feels like to give and receive in balance, to fully live from a compassionate place.

Place your hands over your heart as a gesture of gratitude. Take three slow, deep breaths. Come back to your body and come back to the room. Slowly open your eyes.

ENERGY: WATERFALL

In Chinese medicine it is believed that whatever part of the body is elevated is stimulated. When you're sitting, standing, walking, or driving it's your head that is the most elevated body part. No wonder your mind is always on and there's constant mental chatter! This posture allows your mind to finally take a rest and your energy to recirculate and regenerate.

With your feet and shins on a chair, knees bent, the rest of your body is on the ground. Visualize your legs as a waterfall. You are reversing your blood flow, drawing it downward and allowing it to pool at your core center. This abdominal region is where energy is cleansed and reinvigorated. And the heart continues to move the blood towards the head and then pumps the blood back up to the feet. You could say this is a bit of a cardio activity as well!

Restorative yoga helps to decrease stress, blood pressure, and anxiety. **The idea is that the body can naturally heal itself if it's given a chance to rest.** You will find more energy the rest of today, a fresh mind at work to solve problems, and a better night's sleep!

> Place your calves and feet up on a chair while your head, torso, and hips rest on the floor. You're welcome to place something on the floor to lay on. You can put your hands on your abdomen, out by your side, or cactus arms—whichever feels more natural and comfortable.

THIS SHOULD IMMEDIATELY FEEL WONDERFUL. If you don't feel completely comfortable, see what adjustments need to be made. Are the backs of your knees supported by the edge of the seat cushion? Do you need a folded sweater to support your neck and head? Are you warm enough?

The goal is to relax. Once you have reached a comfortable and sustainable position, close your eyes, take a few deep breaths, and sink into this delicious posture. Stay for 5-20 minutes.

TIP: Set a gentle alarm for your allotted time or play a relaxing song that is the length of your desired duration. It's hard to fully unwind if you're checking the clock every few minutes.

TIP: Does your mind tend to wander and worry about your to-do list? Try the heart meditation activity again while in this resting posture. Your heart is perfectly poised to offer and receive compassion here.

View yourself with compassion as you watch the 2-minute 'movie' of your day.

☐ Check this box when you've completed your daily Neuroflix!

DAY 9 MOMENT OF Z.E.N.

Today your focus was on compassion. Knowing that everyone is trying their best, it can be useful to give your colleagues and co-workers the benefit of the doubt. Send them compassion, as well as to yourself. Taking some time for a restful posture like Waterfall is also an act of self-compassion. Giving and receiving compassion can be an infinite source of energy!

Notes and Doodles

Doodle what compassion means to you. It could be a definition, a symbol, or personal experience.

Kindness in words creates confidence.
Kindness in thinking creates profoundness.
Kindness in giving creates love.

– Lao Tzu

DAY 10: Generosity

Congratulations on making it to the last day of the Career Cleanse ☺

Over the past 10 days you have learned many techniques, from understanding that your Inner and Outer Worlds are mirrors of each other, to creating a larger sense of time, from using your imagination and playing, to compassion for self and all beings. All of these techniques encourage you to choose a more positive and freeing way to be in this moment. You don't have to let work consume you. You can choose zen anytime!

On your last day of the cleanse, focus on generosity and abundance. **There are two types of mindsets: one that focuses on scarcity and one that focuses on abundance.** If you believe that the world is full of limitations, then your mind will want to hoard or hide resources, your heart will feel constricted and be wary of others, and your actions may come from a place of fear and survival. However, if you believe that the world is full of abundance, your mind will likely be more open to ideas, your heart can be happy for the good fortune of others, and your actions are more likely to come from a place of trust and faith.

DAY 10: GENEROSITY

Which perspective is accurate? Whichever you choose to believe will become your reality.

Diagram from *The Abundance Loop* by Juliana Park

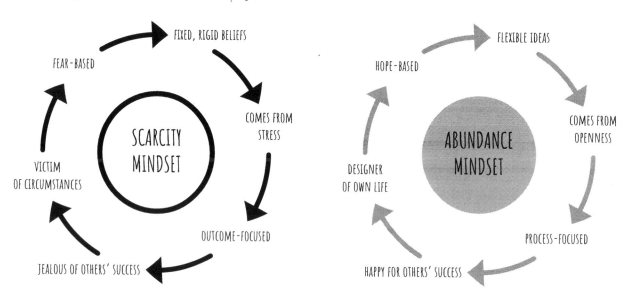

Just like the other techniques you learned, in this moment **you can choose how you want to feel** and how you want to direct your thoughts. As a product of our society, you may have received and internalized the messages of not having enough, not being good enough, wanting to buy more, and needing to be more. Such thoughts feed worries and fears, which can keep you in a tireless loop. But what if you took an opposite approach? What if you chose to believe that you are enough and have enough, and that you're on a journey to continuously evolve and grow? How would that change the way you approach work?

Today choose to be generous and watch what happens. Catch yourself in your belief system — are you coming from a place of scarcity or abundance? Are your actions based on hope or fear?

ZOOM: PAY IT FORWARD

A beautiful way to stay in the flow of abundance and generosity is to pay it forward. This philosophy is based on the cycle of giving and receiving. Everything around you is energy in constant motion, much like plants in nature cycling through life effortlessly. **When you give without the expectation of anything in return, someone else can be the receiver of a genuine gesture**. And then that person can offer a kind gesture to someone else, and so on.

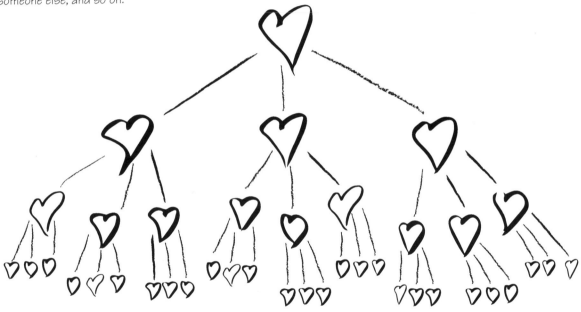

When you stress and strain, however, it impedes the natural rhythm of flow around you. For instance, if you continually overwork yourself, you step out of sync with abundance. You might become physically drained, mentally fried, and/or emotionally resentful of working so much. Being in that depleted Inner World can unfortunately lead to depleted Outer World situations. Seek out opportunities to infuse more fun, lightness, and generosity into your life. Doing so will pay it forward!

DAY 10: GENEROSITY

There are many delightful ways to pay it forward at work.

Here are some easy ideas to get the momentum going:

- Offer someone a sincere compliment
- Pick a flower on your way into work and give it to the first person you see
- Share a cute animal video or funny meme
- Leave a thoughtful gift on your colleague's desk … anonymously
- Hand write a "just because" card to a co-worker
- Bring in healthy treats for everyone and include a copy of the recipe
- Share delicious leftovers from a company party with custodial staff
- Look someone in the eye and give them a kind smile
- Empty out the shredder or tidy up the copy room
- Channel your inner grandparent and offer wisdom to someone in need
- Buy someone a cup of coffee
- Buy someone that you don't know a cup of coffee
- Say a prayer for someone
- Wash the dirty dishes left in the sink

Those are some ideas that don't take a lot of time or money. It's about the thoughtful intention of genuinely caring for others and trying to help someone out. **Your act of generosity can be the start of a beautiful cycle that others will become inspired by.**

ENERGY: SHARE A CUP OF TEA

People have been drinking tea for thousands of years. Folklore says that a farmer in China was resting underneath a tree and drinking a cup of hot water when a few dried leaves fell from the branch above him. Delighted by the fragrance, the farmer began to tell people about this leaf-infused beverage!

Tea is used in rituals and ceremonies, as healing medicine, as well as a means to connect people together. When you drink a hot cup of tea, it can warm the soul and make you feel grounded again. The primal part of you knows that in this moment you are safe and cared for. An immediate sigh of relief might come from that first sip. Those work projects and meetings that seemed so urgent suddenly can wait. **Everything is put in perspective.**

When tea becomes ritual, it takes its place at the heart of our ability to see greatness in small things.

- Muriel Barbery

DAY 10: GENEROSITY

People in Australia and New Zealand enjoy tea and snacks during the "Elevenses," which takes place, as the name implies, around 10 or 11a.m.. It's wonderful to take a mid-morning break, giving you a chance to reflect on your tasks and re-prioritize them as needed. Doing so can prevent you from working through your lunch hours and (erroneously) thinking that "I have to get this done now!" Taking a step back can help you produce mindful, quality work.

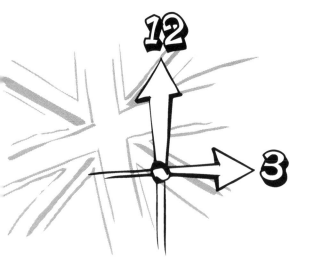

The English are known for their afternoon tea, which is often served around 3 or 4 p.m., and often accompanied by light snacks or sweets. That's another great time of day to rest and reset. You might feel drowsy a little after lunch. Getting up to make a cup of tea can give you valuable reflection time. You can review your day's work so far, see what you've already accomplished (keeping Plan A in mind), and sense what can be addressed tomorrow. This can make the last part of your day really pleasant! **You can leave work feeling accomplished and ready for the next day, rather than the vague and oppressive feeling of there's still so much left to do.**

<u>Today invite someone to share a cup of tea with you</u>. **The act of offering a warm beverage to someone is a beautiful soulful act that is buried deep in your DNA.** In modern-day workplaces, it's nice to go back to a more basic time where it's simply two beings sharing a moment together. So consider whom you'd like to invite to tea today. It could be a co-worker you know well so that you can catch up with them. Or it could be someone with whom you aren't as close, making this is an opportunity to connect in a new way. If you have someone in mind, let them know earlier in the day that you'd like to treat them to a cup of tea. **Double points if you even have some snacks to share!** Colleagues really appreciate this invitation. They perk up and look forward all day to tea time, and their positive energy starts another cycle of giving and receiving. May sharing a cup of tea benefit the both of you to return with a refreshed energy the rest of the day.

Word to the wise: Sometimes people gather at work to vent or complain about others. Have the intention of this shared time as being a positive conversation. Perhaps you discuss a favorite hobby or upcoming trip, favorite places to eat or a great movie you've seen lately. Anything about pets and grand kids usually brings a smile to people's faces!

The act of offering a warm beverage to someone is a beautiful soulful act that is buried deep in your DNA.

Recall how your day went by watching today's 2-minute 'movie.' Enjoy!

☐ Check this box when you've completed your daily Neuroflix!

DAY 10 MOMENT OF Z.E.N.

You are ending your 10-Day Career Cleanse with generosity and paying it forward. Stress and constriction hinder this cycle, so by acting from an open-hearted place you can encourage the continuation of this flow. There are many simple acts you can practice, from sending a thank-you note to sharing a cup of tea. **Thank YOU for initiating this cycle of giving and receiving!**

Notes and Doodles

What actions did you take to demonstrate generosity today? Doodle what that experience felt like.

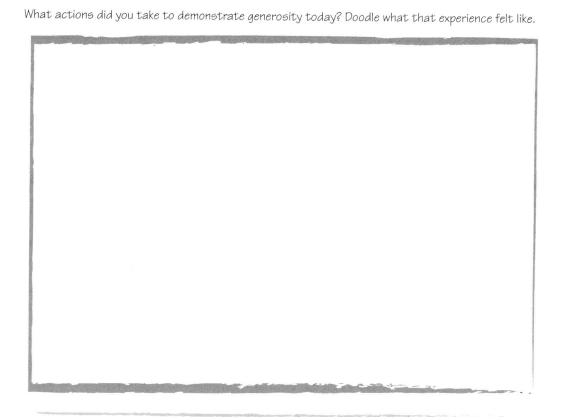

If one advances confidently in the direction of his dreams, and endeavors to live the life which he has imagined, he will meet with a success unexpected in common hours.

- Henry David Thoreau

We shall not cease from exploration,
and the end of all our exploring will be
to arrive where we started and
know the place for the first time.

—T. S. Eliot

CONCLUSION

You have successfully completed the 10 Day Career Cleanse!

You are literally a different person today than you were ten days ago. Cells in your body have been replaced, neural connections in your brain have begun rewiring, your intentions have set forth chains of events, and your collective actions have directly and indirectly impacted everything around you. Wow!

Small changes every day accumulate to great change over time. Creating more zen at work doesn't have to be a laborious process. It can actually be fun and easy! Take a moment and think back to the beginning of this program. What inspired you to start this 10 Day Career Cleanse? How were you feeling then? Look back at that doodle if it helps. Remember what you wanted to clear out and what you wanted to bring in? In the past ten days has anything changed or shifted? By transforming your Inner World with conscious thoughts, feelings, and actions, your Outer World is going to mirror it back to you.

Let your experiences and observations from the last ten days give you information about how to move forward. Continue to explore who you are and what works best for you. Take your favorite parts of this program and create routines that will keep you centered when challenges arise, open to new ideas for problem solving, and relaxed to welcome in more joy.

MOVING FORWARD

You are invited to now create your own daily ritual. Throughout the last ten days you've tried many techniques designed to increase joy and decrease stress. See if you can create a simple system to incorporate them into your workday. **Find your zen at work!**

Recall the three main principles of the program:

 Have fun because joy comes from within.

 Take breaks to relax and release the mental stronghold.

 Do less and get more done. Allow solutions to come to you.

IDENTIFY TECHNIQUES

Which of the 10 Day Career Cleanse techniques helped you to feel less stress, more relaxed, peaceful, playful, and centered? Circle them below. If you noticed an improvement in just ten days, imagine what ten weeks of this would feel like!

	ZOOM	ENERGY	NEUROFLIX
Day 1: Inner World	Intention	Swaying Seaweed	Your Day
Day 2: Create Time	Breathe	Untech Your Neck	Your Day
Day 3: Get Unstuck	Change Gears	Flood Your Cells	Your Day
Day 4: Detach	Be Like Spock	Step Outside	Your Day
Day 5: Imagine	Daydream	Bread & Butter	Your Day
Day 6: Play	Car Talk Humor	Dance	Your Day
Day 7: Allow	Plan A	Power Pose	Your Day
Day 8: Gratitude	Blessing	Love Cloud	Your Day
Day 9: Compassion	Heart Meditation	Waterfall	Your Day
Day 10: Generosity	Pay It Forward	Share a Cup of Tea	Your Day

NEW ROUTINE

Now let's see what your new daily routine might look like. Sketch out a plan that includes your favorite techniques and the ideal times of day. Remember that you don't need to devote hours of wellness at work to see an improvement; it's in the short daily routines where you'll create and maintain the wellness.

Try This: The Daily G.I.V.E.

A simple way to create routine is to have an acronym that serves as a helpful reminder. The one that my clients find most useful is The Daily GIVE.

The acronym of G.I.V.E. is a customizable framework based on your preferred techniques. **The key is to practice this every day at work so that it becomes a new routine for you.**

G = Gratitude, Generosity, or Get Unstuck

Begin your routine with a positive mindset to set the tone for more good things to come.

I = Intention, Imagine, or Inner World

You get to be the architect of your day's unfolding! Choose how you want to feel today.

V = Visualize

Any of the meditations that resonated with you can be your daily guided visualization. You can also use Neuroflix at the end of your day as visualization.

E = Energize

You learned many ways of energizing the body, such as stretching, dancing, walking outside, restorative yoga, and power poses. Keep yourself replenished!

The key is to practice this every day at work so that it becomes a new routine for you.

Commit to your new routine for another 10 days. Make tweaks and notes along the way. Your coworkers, family, or friends might start noticing a positive change in you. Tell them what you're doing to find you zen at work. They'll be so impressed!

You are welcome to repeat this 10-Day Career Cleanse as often as you'd like. You can do it continuously as-is or modify it to include only your favorites. Maybe you choose to repeat this program one technique at a time, making it a 21-day career cleanse. Pick it back up anytime you need a boost of positivity at work. Your life is supposed to be fulfilling and enjoyable to you. Don't wait around for things to get better in order to feel good. **Be proactive and own your zen.**

Day 1	
Day 2	
Day 3	
Day 4	
Day 5	
Day 6	
Day 7	
Day 8	
Day 9	
Day 10	

CONCLUSION

When your life is balanced, all roads lead to the same destination: your highest good, your personal best. You were meant to feel free and empowered, be surrounded by those who celebrate you, continually learn and be challenged, and do fulfilling and meaningful work.

My goal is to start a revolution of happy people at work. There are too many unfulfilled people in their careers. For some, their job may not be a good fit for them. For others it's about replenishment and recharging. For everyone, this is about making changes today that will give you the energy and clarity to make better choices for yourself in the future. Life is too short to be miserable. Make a promise to yourself to summon the zen from within.

Thanks for embarking on this 10 Day Career Cleanse! May this be the beginning of a beautiful and joyful journey for you.

NAMASTE, Y'ALL

Afterword

"No one can steal your joy."

Nearly fifteen years ago, two of my favorite things came together fortuitously: studying yoga and traveling internationally. I had just started a regular yoga practice and was diving deeply into the philosophy and psychology of this Eastern teaching. Applying the concepts of strength, ease, and balance to all facets of my life was fulfilling, especially as I was learning a new job and going through a divorce. Within the serenity of the yoga studios, I found a profound peace born of the wisdom of our teachers and like-minded students. This experience was in stark contrast to the frenzied and crowded airports I frequently found myself in during my travels. Grumpy passengers, worn-down airport workers, and unavoidable delays or cancelled flights—it was a stressfest.

Seeking a little refuge from the whirlwind world of aviation travel, I took solace in the small, tucked-away spots in airports. International terminals are often less busy than their domestic counterparts, and I would watch a movie on my laptop at an empty gate or munch on healthy snacks at a café. But the most surprising find for me was discovering how absolutely quiet and peaceful the airport restroom was. In an unoccupied stall, I claimed my own little space where I could shut out the noise and buzz of the external world and focus on cultivating that "yoga studio" feeling. There I could meditate, stretch, and even dance—anything to find my inner peace again! I realized that yoga and its precepts are applicable literally anywhere. **Soon zenning out in the airport became such a regular thing that I looked forward to that sacred time with each trip that I took.** To my amazement, this airport restroom time became so ingrained in me that I actually came to experience the same zen feeling the moment I walked into any public restroom!

My intentional practice made every restroom a sanctuary to me!

Then it hit me: if this inner peace technique works in restrooms, surely it must work in offices! At the time, I was a full-time university career counselor on large public campus. While I loved my job, the stress of the everyday busyness was starting to wear on me. I had fallen into the trap of trying to get "everything" done. (Truly a hopeless endeavor. There will always be more to do. Always!) After noticing my work stress negatively impacting my health, I decided to refocus my efforts on simply helping my clients, without letting things outside my control bother me. So I began the journey of applying wellness principles to my time in the office. And guess what—it worked!

This book came about because of my serendipitous findings. Who knew an airport restroom would become my inspiration? May you find joy in the most unexpected places in the world!

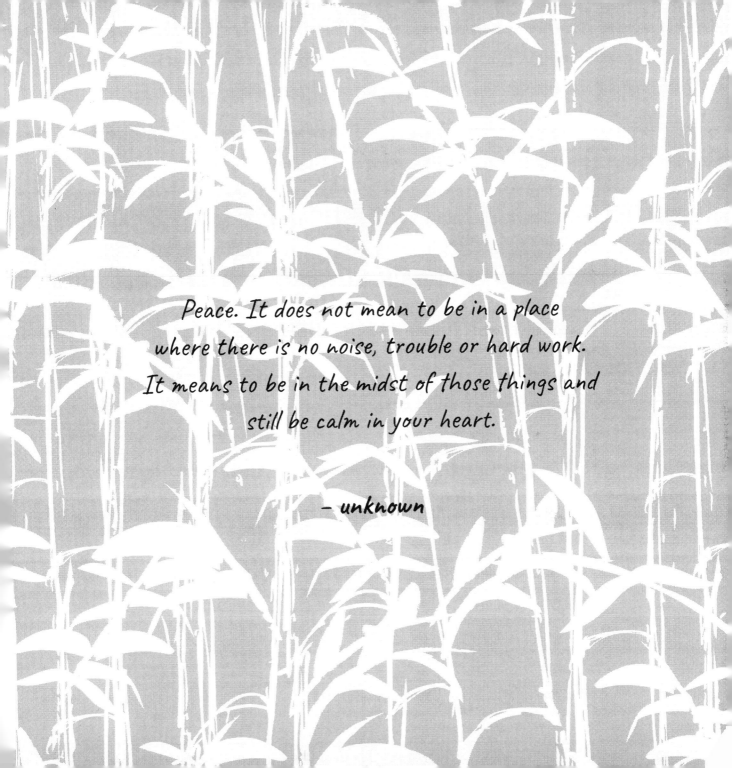

Peace. It does not mean to be in a place
where there is no noise, trouble or hard work.
It means to be in the midst of those things and
still be calm in your heart.

– unknown

Made in the USA
Columbia, SC
27 May 2018